GAYLE H. SWIFT

WITH

CASEY A. SWIFT

ILLUSTRATED BY PAUL GRIFFIN

ABC, Adoption & Me
©2013 by Gayle Swift

Illustrations by Paul Griffin of "Spike's Designs"

WRB Publishing
Palm City, FL 34990
wrb1174@comcast.net

ISBN-13: 978-0-9856762-8-5

www.GIFTfamilyservices.com

Dedicated
To my beloved children,
Casey and Parker,
To their birthparents,
To all adopted children and everyone who loves them,
And to my husband, George

How to Use ABC, Adoption & Me

Adopted families face unique challenges. Curiosity about birth parents and birth family history, feelings of loss, and fears of abandonment are all common. They also can be the source of conflicted, scary emotions. Many adopted children have concerns about permanency and worry about how their parents will react to their questions and fears. Some kids struggle in silence because they want to protect their adopted parents.

Read this book together. Ask your child to identify similarities and differences in her own adoption. Explore her responses and trust her ability to handle her story. Respect the reality of your child's struggle. Avoid minimizing or over-dramatizing any challenges. Provide the strength, acceptance, and security she needs.

Use this book to explore difficult issues with your child. He can overcome these hurdles with you as his safe harbor. Your loving support will help him braid his dual heritage into healthy unity. He will learn to rely on you for comfort and the truth. Understand stormy feelings coexist with love for his adopted family and they do not diminish his connection to it.

Raise adoption conversations with your child. Children think about these issues even if parents never mention them. Some adoptees wait for parents to introduce the conversation first. Let your child know adoption is a safe topic. But, allow her to decide when to continue the conversation. Share age-appropriate, truthful information, especially for difficult or painful facts. Expand the details over time. Be truthful yet diplomatic and sensitive.

Teach your child how to talk about his adoption. Guide him in setting privacy boundaries and choosing with whom he shares his adoption story. Develop your **AQ** (Adoption-attunement Quotient.*) Choose parenting strategies based on adoption-sensitive techniques, like Time-*in* instead of *Time Out*. Be in joy together as you build your lives as an adopted family.

* Adoption-attunement Quotient (AQ,) considers how adoption influences a child. The umbrella of AQ includes:

- ➤ Adoption-sensitive parenting techniques
- ➤ Sound adoption language
- ➤ Knowledge of the attachment process
- ➤ Consideration of grief and loss issues
- ➤ Respect for birth parents
- ➤ Modeling healthy boundaries
- ➤ Educating family, friends and teachers on adoption
- ➤ Remembering that a child's story belongs to him
- ➤ Recognizing that adoption is a family experience
- ➤ Encouraging playfulness and good humor as a family value
- ➤ Integrating a child's birth heritage
- ➤ Parents handle their own grief and loss issues

 is for adoption. Some families come together through adoption, mine did.

B

is for birthdays and belly buttons.
Everyone has one, even adoptees like me!

C is for children. You can be adopted at any age, from tiny babies to teens.

D is for dreams. Sometimes I dream about my birth parents and wonder if they look like me.

 is for EXCITED! That's how my parents felt when they adopted me.

 is for family.

Like all adopted children, I have a birth family.

Some adoptees have foster families. Some lived in orphanages and had friends and special caregivers there.

Adoptive families are forever families.
Both birth and adoptive families are important, permanent parts of us.

G is for group. Children can be adopted in a group with their birth brothers and sisters.

H is for homecoming and heart. Homecoming is the day I joined my adoptive family. My birth family holds a special place in our hearts.

I is for international. I was born in the United States. Some kids are adopted from other countries.

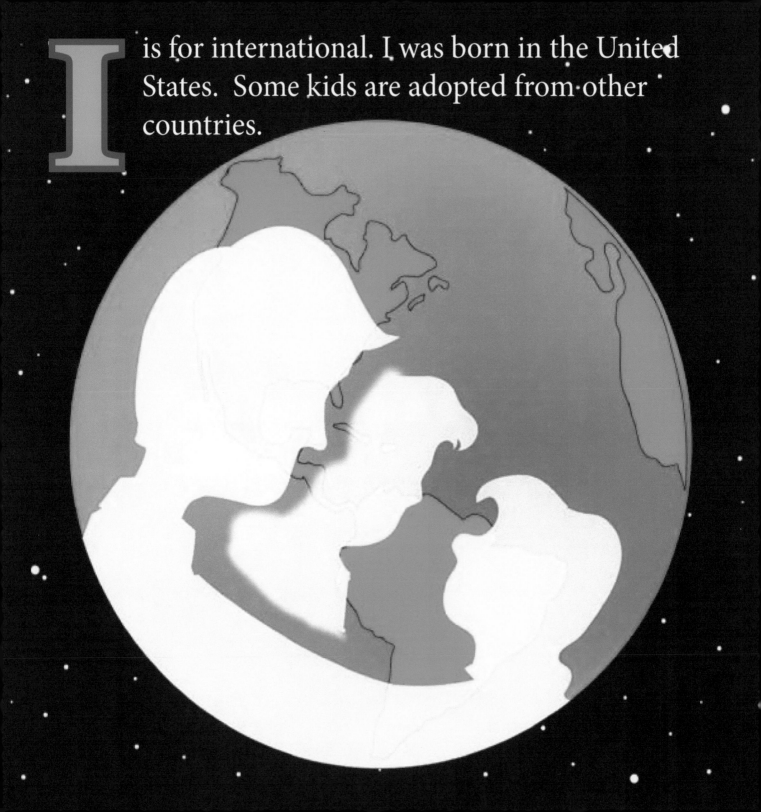

J is for judge. The Judge is the one who makes the adoption official.

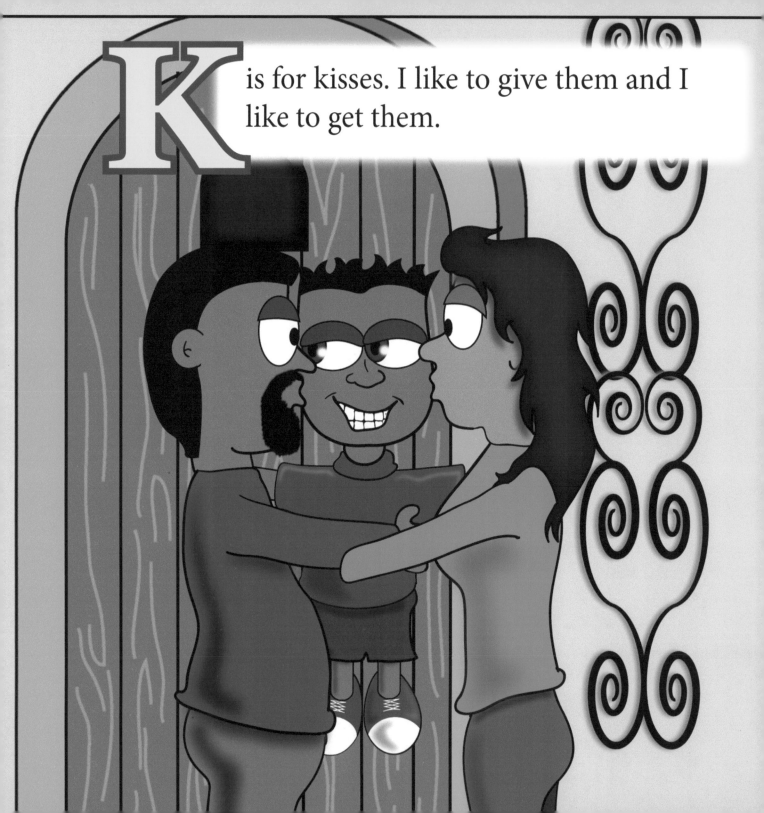

K is for kisses. I like to give them and I like to get them.

L is for love. Our family grew together through love.

M is for miss. Sometimes I miss my birth parents. I wonder if they miss me too.

N is for naughty or nice. When I'm naughty or when I am nice, my parents still love me. I learn from my mistakes.

O is for open adoptions. In open adoptions, adoptees know their birth parents. They visit eac other and spend time together—a little or a lot.

P

is for parents. Birth parents gave me life. Adoptive parents gave me a (forever) family in which to grow up.

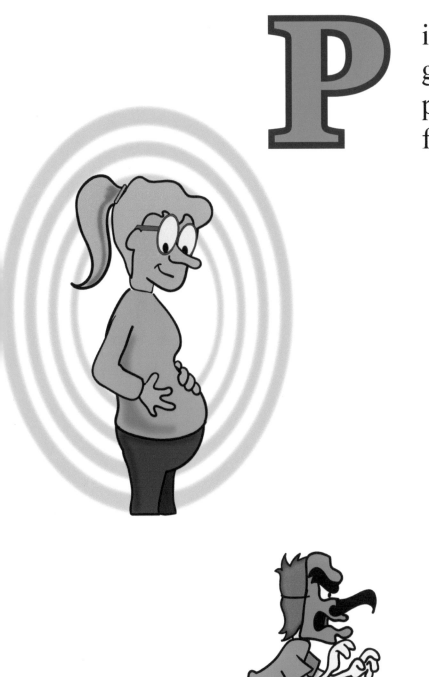

Q is for questions. It's ok to have questions about what being adopted means.

People may ask me about my adoption. I can decide if I want to answer them or not.

R is for real. My birth parents and my adoptive parents are all real. I'm a real kid and we are a real family.

S

is for shapes and sizes. Kids can be adopted by families who look different or the same.

T is for trust and truth. I can trust my parents to tell me the truth about my adoption. We talk about the easy and hard parts too.

U

is for understand. Sometimes it is hard to understand why I was adopted.

V

is for visit. Someday I might get a chance to visit my birth family.

W is for wish. Sometimes I wish my adoptive parents had given birth to me.

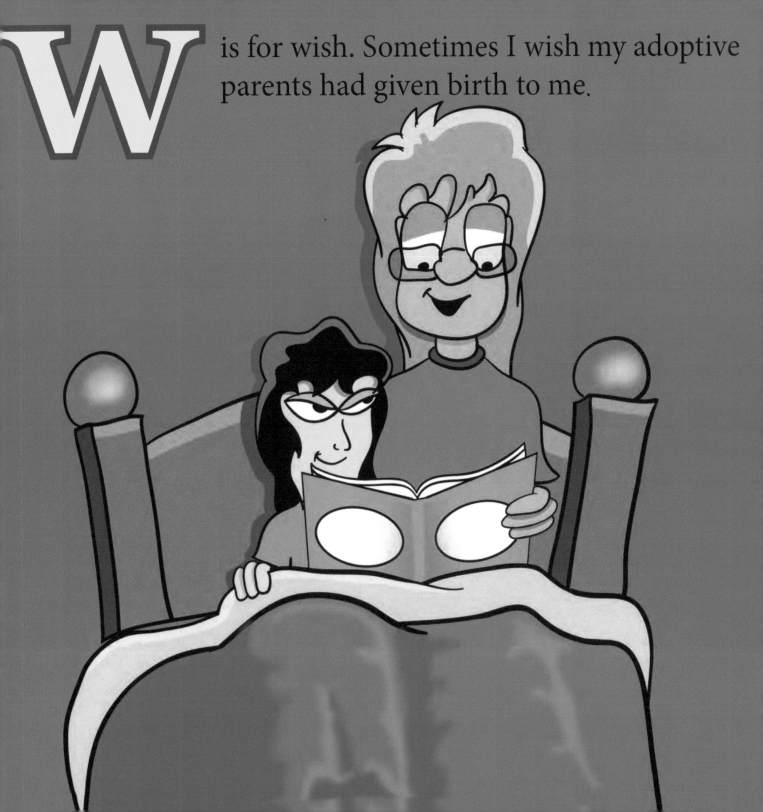

X

is for X's. On letters and cards, they stand for the hugs we share as a family.

 is for you. Families treasure what makes you one-of -a-kind special.

Z is for zig zag. Sometimes I feel happy and sad about being adopted.

Authors and Illustrator

ward-winning author Gayle H. Swift drew on her experience as an adoptive parent, adoption coach and foster parent to create *ABC, Adoption & Me*. Co-founder of GIFT Family Services, she is dedicated to supporting adoptees and the families who love them.

asey Anne Swift, adoptee, teacher, and co-author of *ABC, Adoption & Me*, collaborated with her mother on this project. Together, they have created a book designed to support and encourage adoptees as they travel their adoption journey.

aul Griffin, owner of "Spike's Designs" illustrated *ABC, Adoption & Me*. Paul thoroughly enjoyed collaborating with both authors to bring the message of love, acceptance and understanding to support adoptees and their families. Paul also illustrated *The Family Zoo* which shares this message.

CPSIA information can be obtained
at www.ICGtesting.com
Printed in the USA
BVHW021559020919
557363BV00004B/91/P